MESSY & FOOLISH

How to Make a Mess, Be a Fool, and Evangelize the World

MATTHEW WARNER

DynamicCatholic.com
Be Bold. Be Catholic.®

Printed in the United States of America. [1]

ISBN: 978-1-942611-77-6

Design by: Rachel Lee

For more information on bulk copies of this title or other
books and CDs available through the Dynamic Catholic
Book Program, please visit www.DynamicCatholic.com
or call 859-980-7900.

The Dynamic Catholic Institute
5081 Olympic Blvd • Erlanger • Kentucky • 41018
Phone: 1–859–980–7900
Email: info@DynamicCatholic.com

THESE
WORDS
ARE
SHARED
HERE
FOR
ANYONE
FOOLISH
ENOUGH
TO
READ
THEM.

TABLE OF CONTENTS

INTRODUCTION:

The Problem (and the Goal)

PART ONE:

On Messes (and Thinking Differently about Them)

PART TWO:

On Foolishness (and What It Looks Like)

PART THREE:

On Evangelizing the World (When and How to Do It)

THE PROBLEM

(and the Goal)

There were no pews or seats, only cold, wet sand. But that wasn't going to stop three million energetic young people from celebrating Mass that day on Copacabana Beach in Brazil.

"Go!" said Pope Francis. "You have been able to enjoy the wonderful experience of meeting Jesus, meeting him together with others, and you have sensed the joy of faith. But the experience of this encounter must not remain locked up in your life or in the small group of your parish, your movement, or your community."

As the 2013 World Youth Day festivities came to a close, the pope was kicking everyone out — but not without marching orders.

"I want a mess. I want trouble in the dioceses! I want people to go out! I want the Church to go out into the streets! I want us to defend ourselves against everything that is worldliness, installation, comfortableness, clericalism, being shut in on ourselves. The parishes, the schools, the institutions exist to go out!"

IT'S TIME TO MAKE A MESS

When you know you have something really special, you can't help but want to share it with everyone you meet. And when that something happens to be God's honest truth — the gospel, the secret to a meaningful and joyful life — you'd think it would be spreading like wildfire.

But it's not spreading like wildfire. In fact, the fire seems to be going out. We must be doing something wrong.

In the next generation, half the pews will empty. And not because of something that will happen, but because of something that has happened. A generation is already missing and so are their children. And they show no signs of coming back any time soon. The inertia alone ensures that the situation will get worse before it gets better. It's a crisis of massive proportions, the severity of which has been masked by positive personal anecdotes and clouded in an ambiguous "hope" that, in the end, things will turn out fine anyway.

Sure, we can point to many bright spots worth celebrating within the Church today, but the bleeding continues. None have yet reversed the mass exodus of modern man from church.

We're in the midst of an identity crisis. We've forgotten we were made to live courageously. We've forgotten who we are. We've forgotten we've been charged with a radical mission — a mission to turn the world on its head.

There is indeed hope. But it's not a vague, passive hope, where we stand on the sidelines and wait for God to swoop in. Rather, it's a hope intimately tangled up in our human messiness and fueled by our weakness. It's a fool's hope.

It is time for big, bold changes. It's time to get out of maintenance mode and go on a mission. It's time to *go*! You exist to go out, to be shared, to love and be loved. The Church exists to engulf all of humanity, not just the poor sinners within its walls. But unfortunately, whatever we're doing now simply isn't working.

There is a movement afoot, though — a movement that, by God's grace, can turn the tide.

It is a movement of people inspired by the opportunity of the information age, prompted by the poverties of modernity, and frustrated by the status quo. It is a movement fueled by big ideas and an exciting vision for the Church. A movement of people who know that the dawn of a new renaissance is possible in our lifetime.

These people are already hard at work, through many diverse efforts across the country, as faithful partners in this new evangelization. And more people are joining this movement every day.

But what makes their evangelization efforts so successful when so many others are failing? The secret is that they begin where we must all begin — with a mess and a fool.

Are you concerned that the genius of Christianity is not being taken seriously? Are you as frustrated as I am that so many continue to walk away from it without ever really knowing it? Are you ready to start a new era of evangelization unlike the world has ever seen? Good. Now let's get started.

Pope Francis was right. It's time to make a mess. It's time to change the world. And we are just the fools to do it.

WHAT NEEDS TO CHANGE

As Christians, we spend a lot of time working to improve the world in various ways. For example, we work hard for peace and justice — clothing the naked, feeding the hungry and serving those in need. We want to make the world a better place and give people hope.

But, of course, our work for peace and justice is much more profound than simply social change, fixed problems, and good feelings. Our end goal is not just to change the world, but, through that work, to change the way people *see* the world.

This distinction is subtle, but crucial. By changing the way people see the world, we change how they see themselves. This shift in perspective is what opens people up to reconsider the facts they may have disregarded in the past. Evangelistic efforts that lead with finely reasoned arguments, before first allowing somebody the chance to see the world differently, rarely work. Once people develop a strongly held belief, it is not usually initially changed by the facts. If we want the facts to make a difference, we need to inspire people to consider a new perspective first.

Christianity has a very specific vision for how we should see the world and ourselves — a vision of man fully alive. But modern minds are skeptical. They don't take us seriously. God wants to give every single person a great life of literally never-ending joy, and yet so many remain unconvinced.

"We are half-hearted creatures," wrote C. S. Lewis, "fooling about with drink and sex and ambition when infinite joy is offered us, like an ignorant child who wants to go on making mud pies in a slum because he cannot imagine what is meant by the offer of a holiday at the sea. We are far too easily pleased."[1]

Our proposal to the world — our invitation — is to see the world differently, to trade the mud pies for that holiday at the sea, for true freedom and lasting peace.

When clearly presented, who could refuse such an invitation?

So our purpose — your purpose — is to help the God of the universe change the world by helping others to see the world differently. That is, to help them see the truth about who made them and there discover their true identity and purpose. Whether you're a mother, father, brother, sister, teacher, farmer, leader, builder, thinker, doer, doodler, dawdler, or whatever, your purpose involves nothing short of helping the God of the universe help the world to see. That's evangelization.

This is especially true in raising our children. We're not just equipping them to become faithful cogs in the industrial machine, safely navigating life's pitfalls. We're not just helping them to survive this life or even ultimately to "succeed." We are here to teach our children to see the world differently — to discover a loving God who made us all to live big, beautiful, meaningful lives.

And regarding your membership in the Church, you have certainly not been tasked with perpetuating the status quo. You are not here to merely maintain a great institution and to keep people from leaving it. Such is the posture of a dying organization.

No! You exist to boldly carry the torch handed down to us by our radical founder, Jesus. Your duty is to upend all that is backward in the world by joyfully setting it aflame with the true, the good, and the beautiful.

So how do we do all this? How do we set the world aflame? How do we reverse the mass exodus? How do we convince the unconvinced? How do we change the way people see the world?

First, we need to make a mess. But before we get started, there are some important things we must learn about messes.

PART ONE

ON MESSES

(and Thinking Differently
about Them)

MESSES CAN BE GOOD

The steps leading up to our mudroom were covered in empty boxes, piles of tools, and bags of household items to be given away. I could barely open the door due to even more boxes, a mound of old shoes, a broom, and a bag of clothes behind it. When I finally made my way through the clutter, I found my beautiful wife, her hair piled atop her head and a dustpan in her hand.

I pulled her in for a hug and helped her put another bag by the door, grateful for the temporary mess she had made. I knew all of our closets and cabinets and rooms were now less cluttered and more functional because of the mess that was made to rearrange them.

After all, when things aren't put together quite right, they need to be jumbled around. They need to be thought about entirely differently. They need to be taken apart, spread across the floor, dusted off, and put back together better.

So sure, generally we think of messes as bad things. And generally, that's probably true. After all, our God is a god of order. But sometimes a mess can be good.

HOW TO MAKE A GOOD MESS

In 1908, when Henry Ford introduced the first mass-market automobile, the Model T, he made a real mess of the horse-and-buggy industry. But it was a helpful mess that increased mobility, improved quality of life, and connected people like never before.

A century later we entered the Information Age, a paradigm shift in how we communicate and share information. Taking advantage of this new technology means changing the way things have been done for a long time. It means trying something new. It's a messy, uncomfortable process but often necessary and good.

And it's not just technology that creates good, disruptive messes.

Martin Luther King Jr. had a dream and acted on it despite danger and risk. He made a complete mess of the way a lot of people saw the world, and he changed it for the better.

Even the Creator of the universe likes a good mess. While our world is certainly marked by an amazing order, it's also messy. It's wild. Just look at the food chain, the formation of mountains, the waves hitting the shore. Nature is constantly creating and destroying in an unpredictable and necessary fashion. It's messy and wild, just like our lives.

But perhaps nobody made a mess quite like another guy who was born two thousand years ago, a man who made this crazy claim that he was God and that he was the way, the truth, and the life. He disrupted the social order, healed on the Sabbath, forgave sins, befriended outcasts, and founded his own religion. He allowed himself to be misunderstood, tortured, and killed. And to top it off, he left a simple, flawed fisherman in charge of the whole thing.

God could have revealed himself to us in numerous ways. He could have explained himself nicely and neatly. But he knew that the only way to really get through to us was to make an absolute mess of things. So he turned all of our own disordered systems, twisted desires, selfish ambitions, and arbitrary expectations completely upside down.

God loves a good mess if it helps us get the message. And he's OK with things breaking sometimes, especially when it allows him to break through to us.

In a world where the status quo is so massively failing, these are the kinds of messes we need to make today — big, bold, good messes.

THE WORK OF AN ARTIST

Anybody can make a mess. But making a *good* mess requires the work of an artist — and you are the artist.

Now, by "artist" I don't mean only the obvious kinds, such as painters, sculptors, and musicians. I mean something much more profound.

Art, in this deeper sense, is simply the expression or application of human creative skill and imagination. It's the work of applying our creativity and imagination to the world, to our jobs, and to our lives. This is art. And you, in everything you do — especially in your work to change the world — are an artist.

So was Mother Teresa. She was a masterful artist. She saw the world in a special way, and she communicated that through her radical service to others. That was her art.

Steve Jobs was an artist. He had a vision for how the world could be different, and he communicated that through elegant, new technology. That was his art.

Whether saint, innovator, or ordinary worker, we are all artists. After all, we are made in the image of the Great Artist himself.

Artists create and connect. They create something — a product, a doohickey, a program, a party, a painting, an idea, a new method, anything you can imagine. And then through that they communicate something to other people. Their idea, party, or product changes the way someone sees the world.

Isn't this precisely the work of the Church? This is evangelization — the work of changing the world and the way people see it.

Unfortunately, like so many other dimensions of our lives, our evangelizing has lost its artistic touch. Whether it's how we take care of the poor, educate our children, manage our relationships, or pass on the faith, our industrial, hyper-productive minds have come to depend deeply on The System. We'd rather have a programmatic society managed by distant representatives that runs with little personal effort, correcting itself as we sleep, leaving us free to indulge our individualism. The Industrial Kingdom was born of laboratories, assembly lines, and mass production, so why not her subjects, too? Surely solving our problems must simply be a matter of having the right policies, cramming process and people in one end and popping perfectly formed and faithful citizens out the other?

But it just doesn't work that way in the wild. We need artful evangelists, not industrial evangelists. Evangelization is an art more than a science. It's not merely the logistical challenge of disseminating fact, but a dangerous adventure in loving each other.

We need artists who are ready to get messy.

God, the Great Artist, is asking us to share his vision for the world. He's asking us to see the world differently — that is, as he sees us. And he sees us as artists, full and active participants in the continued creation of the world.

We produce and form his children. We build his kingdom. And we do so, by his grace, through all of our creative endeavors that change the world. We are co-creators. We are made to create. This is the work of artists, and it is our work.

WHERE IT ALL BREAKS DOWN

As artists, we love the creative part. We love making things. We love dreaming big and imagining that anything is possible! That part is fun. Where most art breaks down, though, is in the sharing of it.

When you have to share your ideas — your *self* — with someone else, you must become vulnerable. You must open yourself up to rejection and criticism. It's scary. But too often that fear turns us into walking facades, mere shadows of the glorious personalities within.

This is what cripples most people's art. It's what cripples most people's careers and relationships. It's what is crippling the Church's evangelistic efforts. And it's what is keeping us from living a life fully alive.

Do you ever really feel more alive than when you are vulnerable? Whether it comes through loving another person or testing a creative idea, you feel life surge through you — all the nerves, emotions, adrenaline, anticipation, and wonder rush through you at that moment when it connects with somebody on the other side.

What will they say? What will they do?

That's living a life fully alive. You were made to do it.

Are you currently doing the work of an artist? What are you creating? How is it helping someone else to see the world differently? And are you being vulnerable? Are you taking a risk? Getting criticized? Learning, repeating, moving forward in faith with the full confidence that knows Christ has already won?

Do not be afraid to share who you really are — especially your flaws and your baggage. These are assets, not liabilities, when it comes to evangelization. God wants to bring great good from your brokenness. Let him.

We must not be afraid to expose our weakness, for it is a great strength. We must not be afraid to fail and make mistakes, both as a Church and as individuals. We must not be afraid to stand up to the challenges in our community. To stand up for truth. To try new approaches. To be humble enough to learn from others. To be human. To show our brokenness and inadequacy. To be authentic. To be vulnerable. It's the only way to make the good messes that still need making.

Yet, the fullest answer to making a mess and evangelizing the world lies deeper still and much, much closer to home.

WHERE THE MESS MUST START

A newspaper once posed the question, "What's wrong with the world today?" Here is one of the replies:

Dear Sirs,

I am.

Yours,

G. K. Chesterton[2]

The mess making must start with us, in our own hearts. We must make a mess of our own confused priorities, all the things we love more than God but pretend we don't.

We can talk about the importance of catechesis, community, leadership, orthodoxy, the sacraments, and the fullness of truth. We can complain about politics and how we need more preaching from the pulpit. We can blame it on everything else wrong in the world. But here is the reality, the real reason people do not take the Christian invitation seriously:

We Christians don't look or act all that different from non-Christians. It's that simple.

If Christianity offers a better way, why aren't more people attracted to living that life?

If we believe our faith and action in this life have eternal consequences, why don't we live like it? If the God of our universe, the Creator of everything, truly gives us his body and blood, why don't we act like it?

If our relationship with God is truly the most important relationship, why don't our daily schedules reflect that? If our marriages and families are our greatest blessings, why do we sacrifice them for our careers?

If God has a plan for us, why do we make so many plans without him? Why are we not on our knees every morning thanking, praising, and trusting him with every moment of our entire day?

If we truly believe he has conquered the world, why are we so afraid to just be ourselves?

If Christianity is true, why isn't everything we do ordered around this truth?

The incongruity between what we claim to believe and the lives we live says everything the world needs to know. Any honest outsider can tell that we can't possibly believe what we say we believe. Not only is our religion a fraud, but so are we Christians. At least, that's what our actions often communicate to the world.

This was summed up half a century ago by the Second Vatican Council, which said: "One of the gravest errors of our time is the dichotomy between the faith which many profess and the practice of their daily lives."[3] It's not a new challenge.

So, my friends, if we are waiting for the institutional Church to stem the tide and fix this problem, if we're waiting for it to evangelize the world, we're missing the point.

Sure, we need inspirational leadership. We need solid teaching. Our organizations need to be more professional. We need to do community and fellowship better. Our leaders need to understand investment and ROI. They need to be more accountable, less wasteful, and less bureaucratic. We should operate with excellence in all things because excellence itself is a Christian thing. And along the way we should embrace all things that are true, good, and beautiful and that serve the mission of the Church, no matter where we find them.

But these things will not solve our problems by themselves, because they are missing a necessary ingredient: you.

We like to hide behind our big institutional solutions to problems. That's why we'd rather elect somebody to clean up the streets than take a walk down our own street with some paint and a broom. That's why we're more likely to pay higher taxes to support the elderly than to spend time getting to know them. And it's why we're more likely to drop ten dollars in the collection plate than we are to take a homeless man to lunch. We love to subsidize and outsource our charity and the fixing of our problems.

Likewise, we like to dream about big ideas, flashy marketing campaigns, large crowds, and innovative programs. We busy and distract ourselves with such efforts, all the while ignoring and avoiding the plain, hard answer staring us in the face every morning when we wake up and look in that mirror.

I know the answer. I just don't like the answer. The mess making must start in my own heart.

What's wrong with the world? I am.

PART TWO

ON FOOLISHNESS

(and What It Looks Like)

WHY BE A FOOL?

For the foolishness of God is wiser than men.

— *St. Paul (1 Corinthians 1:25)*

People can find well-run, professional, inspiration-al organizations and great communities anywhere. But is that what Christ gave us his Church for — to convert the world simply by our operational excellence?

Was the world meant to know us first by our perfect execution, huge budgets, and impressive abilities? Was that God's plan for how the Church would win the world for him? Is that the plan Jesus gave the Twelve Apostles — to win the world by their personal and institutional greatness?

I think not. Jesus knew better, of course.

What is going to win the world first is not our greatness, but our foolishness. It's the world looking at us and saying:

Those fools! They continue to fail and fall, but they keep getting back up.

Those fools! They are willing to look silly, sound crazy, admit failure, take responsibility and be honest about their flaws. They are willing to sacrifice immediate pleasures and comfortable living for something they can't even touch or fully explain.

Those fools, serving others not only from their surpluses but also from their needs — laboring long and working for little.

Those fools! They go to all that trouble and effort over the tiniest of lives and worry about how the already dying happen to die.

That fool, giving up a promotion in order to be home on time for dinner each day.

Those fools! Look how in success they give credit to others and in failure are the first to own responsibility.

That fool, spending hours a day at prayer when he could be more productive instead.

Those fools! They have hope for even the most hopeless and time for the lowest of the lowest.

The world keeps mistreating them and rejecting them and persecuting them, yet it only seems to fuel their fire. Though sometimes it seems everyone is against them, they are the most joyful people we've ever met.

Those fools! See how they forgive even the worst of transgressors. And not just once, but over and over and over again.

Those fools! See how they love even their enemies.

There is something different about these fools. What do they know that we don't? Where does their joy and their peace and their strength and this unwavering love come from? How can we have what they have?

That, my friends, is what will win souls — not our greatness, but our foolishness.

It's a foolishness that only makes any sense at all once you know the secret — the Way, the Truth, and the Life. That is, once you know Jesus.

Some of the greatest evidence of Jesus' rising from the dead is the foolishness that followed. If Jesus did not rise from the dead, that following century (as well as the subsequent two thousand years) makes absolutely no sense. What else could explain the utter foolishness of such a large, fast-growing movement of first-century humans going to the ends of the earth to spread a nonviolent message that would certainly gain them death? What but the risen Jesus?

Furthermore, in the Church's infancy, when the need to evangelize was most critical, the Church didn't grow due to the attractiveness of its programs and Sunday services. It didn't grow because of its operational excellence or the practical wisdom imparted through its monthly talk series. And it certainly didn't grow because of how convenient or easy it was to join and participate.

On the contrary, the Church grew first because of the radical witness of its members, who cared for people nobody else cared for and who made radical personal sacrifices in the ways they lived their lives. It grew because of the way they loved not just their neighbors, but their enemies. Because of how they loved life and didn't fear death. Because of their apparent foolishness.

And only then, as a result of such radical witness, did these Christians come together via the simple ritual established for worship by their founder — for the reading of the Word and the celebration of Eucharistic Communion each Sunday.

The wisdom of the world is no match for the foolishness of God.

A FOOL'S HEART

Fatherhood, for me, has been a wonderful study of human nature.

In raising my four beautiful children, I am reminded of what motivates all of us. My five-year-old son is obsessed with truth, always challenging me with thoughtful questions, trying to make sense of the world and often asking: "Is that *really true*, Dad?" My daughters can't help but dance and twirl when they hear beautiful music. And all my children are attracted most to the people around them who are full of life and joy.

In all these things, I see firsthand the truth of Pope Benedict's words: "Life is not just a succession of events or experiences. It is a search for the true, the good, and the beautiful. It is to this end that we make our choices; it is for this that we exercise our freedom; it is in this — in truth, in goodness, and in beauty — that we find happiness and joy."[4]

In recent decades, the Church has struggled to convincingly share many of its countercultural teachings. We've struggled to show the truth, goodness, and beauty of our beliefs. We've given the impression that Christianity is based upon a bunch of negative rules that tell you only what you can't do in life. This is a sad misunderstanding.

The truth is that the function of every *no* in Christianity is to provide us the freedom to say yes to something better, something more beautiful! And naturally, our faith is considerably more attractive when we talk about it in terms of the corresponding positive points rather than the negative — when we talk about our faith in terms of what we are for rather than what we are against. This is an approach referred to as "affirmative orthodoxy." And it's an important lesson, but it's not enough.

Our approach must go beyond a simply affirmative orthodoxy to an *active* orthodoxy. Our faith must be more than just affirmative; it must also be acted out and genuinely alive in us.

We see this deficiency everywhere. How often is love preached with hostility? Truth told in uncharity? Joy proclaimed blandly?

My parents' generation left the Church without leaving the pews. And now they wonder why their kids find it silly to stand in the pews of a church they never really understood professing creeds they never really believed.

So now we find ourselves scrambling for ways to teach the truth, to instruct the ignorant. We demand orthodoxy. We anguish over so many leaving something they never truly knew. But we go about it all wrong. We attack all the symptoms without really getting to the heart of the matter, to what motivates all of us, including our children.

Instead of lecturing people about going to church on Sunday, let's inspire them to want to go. Instead of telling them to dress more appropriately for Mass, let's give them something worth dressing up for. Instead of telling them not to sleep around, let's fascinate them with the pursuit of purity. Instead of preaching that giving is better than receiving, let's just give.

In other words, instead of talking about how beautiful the faith is, let's show the world its beauty. Instead of insisting how good the Church is, let's *be* good. Instead of lecturing about truth, let's live a life transformed by it.

We have fallen in love with knowing we are right and called it "loving our neighbor." Some of us are guilty of using the truth as a selfish weapon. We use it to hurt people and assert our own rightness (and their wrongness). We use it harshly to win arguments and then call it "tough love."

That's not tough love.

Tough love is daring to meet someone where they are. It's scooping them up and getting your hands dirty with them. Tough love is being in an uncomfortable, dangerous place along their side and daring to slay their dragons together.

It's diving into the deep and terrible things that torment them, holding their hand and fighting your way out together. It's inconvenient, requires you to sacrifice, and seldom involves a lecture or the winning of an argument. Such arguments rarely change hearts, but more often serve to further divide us and puff up our own egos. The world is in desperate need of some tough love, but that is certainly not it. That's cheap love — which means it's not love at all.

Sometimes we act like being orthodox (meaning "right belief" or "right opinion") means making sure — with radical zealotry — that everyone else is following the rules. Meanwhile, we embrace the same for ourselves with an enthusiasm more akin to a child eating broccoli.

It's one thing to profess and enforce a belief. It's another to let it transform your life.

We forget that being a true Christian is not really about having the right opinions; it's about having the right heart — which is a very different thing. An orthodox life is not the mental challenge of staying between the lines, but an exercise in wildly over-flowing the boundaries of the heart. Jesus' love is not measured and controlled. It is total and wild.

That is what active orthodoxy should look like. Our religion, as G. K. Chesterton says, should be less of a theory and more of a love affair.[5]

Don't get me wrong. All the rules and doctrines are essential. In fact, following them is the secret to being set free to love madly without worry of going astray. But they are just the beginning.

In the end, you don't have to beat people over the head with the truth, with an invitation to a holiday at the sea. You just have to open them up to it. Show them the truth, the goodness, the beauty. Help them to see things differently. Convince them — through trust, relationship, and love — to look at something from a new perspective.

Prepare the way, then get out of the way. Open the cage door and let the Truth speak for itself. It will roar like a lion who, once encountered, needs no help being taken seriously.

WHAT WE NEED

As he was walking by the Sea of Galilee, he saw two brothers, Simon who is called Peter, and his brother Andrew, casting a net into the sea; they were fishermen. He said to them, "Come after me, and I will make you fishers of men." At once they left their nets and followed him. (Matthew 4:18–20)

What we need today, just as at that seaside encounter, are people radical and foolish enough to drop their nets at once and follow him. We need people who will do anything for God. *Anything.*

What the Church needs is saints. And saints are not cranked out as nice, neat widgets by well-oiled institutions. They are birthed out of a messy world and inspired by a foolishness that transcends it.

The great thing about saints is that they will not lose their faith because of bad liturgical music. They can suffer bad preaching, small budgets, poor management, and every single one of the many fools we have in this hospital for sinners. They'll still be in the pews on Sunday, quietly winning the world for Christ, slowly transforming the Church, recruiting more saints and often fixing other problems in the process.

Saints are compelling in every age and from every angle. They need few words to be understood. They need no defense. They need no money, gimmicks, glory, or fame. They have but to be authentically themselves, and the world can't help but change.

The world can't help but see things differently.

Saints are the best teachers, too, because the best teachers lead by example. People will learn more from what you do than from anything you will ever say. We've forgotten this when it comes to changing the world.

My grandfather wisely taught me that you don't teach the faith so much as you catch it — like the flu. The faith must never be imposed, but rather allowed to germinate within the natural, messy course of a loving human relationship. But it will only be contagious, of course, to the extent that you yourself have caught it!

Pope Francis points out that "the Church grows by attraction, not proselytizing."[6] The beauty in the Church is irresistible. The problem is that our sin distorts it. The saints learn to magnify that beauty through their love and humility, rather than distort it with proselytizing and pride.

We need saints. And not just saints of the past — *your* sainthood.

When the world sees you, it doesn't have to see a saint yet, but at least let it see a sinner set on sainthood. We shouldn't need to tell people we're Christian. It should be obvious, not by how we label ourselves, but by the lives we live. They should sense Christ radiating authentically, lovingly, and naturally from every move we make. If they can't, we need to stop talking about what's wrong with everyone else and start living a more compelling life.

Saints spread the faith like wildfire because they are willing to catch themselves on fire first. It's that simple. We need an army of saints willing to live a radical life for Christ and others, willing to be fools for Christ and make a mess of their own hearts.

Before the apostles ever preached a word to anyone else, they had the courage to drop their own nets first — not hypothetically, not just sort of, but immediately, totally, and for good. They went all in. Before they asked others to do so, they had the guts to set themselves on fire first.

You don't have to be brilliant. You just have to be brave.

THE RADICAL LIFE

Can you imagine what twelve more Mother Teresas would do for this world? If twelve more people gave Christ 100 percent of their hearts 100 percent of the time and held nothing back, absolutely nothing?
— Peter Kreeft[7]

If we want others to take Christianity seriously — that is, if we want to change the way they see the world — then we must first take it seriously ourselves. That means making radical changes to the way we live our lives. We need more people to answer the call to holiness. All of us have been called to live this radical life — to be saints.

But it won't happen by accident. Each day you must make the courageous choice for yourself.

We humans are made to choose. This is what gives our lives so much purpose. We are here to make important choices. The problem is that we're so busy that we perpetually put off such choices for just one more day . . . and life quickly passes us by.

It's all too easy to mindlessly fill our lives with noisy distractions and busy ourselves with endless activities. We find ourselves simply reacting to a never-ending stream of stimulations, constantly tied up with the urgent and never quite getting to the important. Rather than seizing the day, the day seems to be seizing us! We often feel overwhelmed and helpless, hopelessly held captive by the circumstances of our lives.

But we aren't helpless. The reason we feel this way is that we refuse to choose. We refuse to choose one activity over another, so we try to do both. We refuse to choose one priority over another, leaving us with no priorities at all. We refuse to deny one want over another, so we find ourselves impossibly committed. We refuse to choose the courageous option, settling for the safe move instead.

We refuse to choose a quiet moment of contemplation at the beginning of our day where we decide what we will do today and what we will let go. We refuse to choose between our plans and God's plan. We want it all.

But we can't have it all. And if we could, life would be boring anyway. Part of what makes life sweet is the sacrifice — giving up something good for something better, trading in the mud pies for the holiday at the sea. Deep down we know we should do it, but we don't. It seems too crazy, or too hard, or we're just scared of what people will think.

But you must do it anyway. You were made to do it. You were made to live intentionally. You were made to choose how you live your life, not to let life simply happen to you. If life is just happening to you, then you're caught up in the mire and mediocrity of accidental living. An accidental life will never be fulfilling to a creature that was made to choose.

We were made to make big, courageous choices. So why do we so rarely make them? Why do so few people manage to live this radical life?

TIME
TO DANCE

Sure, we live in a "free society," where we generally spend our days doing whatever we want. But are we really free? After all, freedom is not the ability to do what you want. It's the ability *to say no* to what you want. Only once you are able to say no to what you want are you free to do as you should. Only then are you truly free.

How attached we are to material things. How addicted to good feelings. How needy we are of praise. How desperate for our own power. How accustomed we are to having every want satisfied instantly.

That's why this radical life is so hard to choose and why so few choose it: We are too enslaved to our own wants.

What material things are you most attached to? Give them away. What good feelings are you addicted to? Fast from them. What honors do you most enjoy? Let somebody else enjoy them. What position of authority or power are you most desperate for? Let it go.

It's not the material things that are holding you back, but your attachment to them. It's not the good feelings, but your addiction to them. In fact, these may all be good things in your life, and it's perhaps unimaginable that you would give them up, but that's exactly why they are keeping you from doing something extraordinary with this one wild and precious life[8] of yours.

At this moment, you already have everything you need to do everything God is asking of you. So why aren't you doing it yet? William Law summed up the hard truth well when he said, "If you will look into your own heart in complete honesty, you must admit that there is one and only one reason why you are not a saint: you do not wholly want to be."[9]

You can't just *want* to be a saint. You have to want it with your whole being. You have to want it more than anything else. You have to be willing to sacrifice any other desires that get in your way. Only in such tremendous sacrifice will you be free to live the radical life God created you to live.

Are you willing to start making these sacrifices, even when everyone else is scared to? Even when everyone else will think you foolish?

It only takes one fool to fill an empty dance floor — just one poor soul, free from the cares of what other people think, with the courage to start dancing. For his dancing ends not in ridicule, but in more fools dancing.

PART THREE

ON EVANGELIZING THE WORLD

(When and How to Do It)

WHEN YOU CAN START

It's a scary, powerful thing to realize that at this very moment you can decide to change your life forever. The life you were made to live can be yours right now if you have the courage to choose it.

You must act now, though. When it comes to matters of sainthood, the answer is always now. Not after you make a little more money, or after you get that promotion, or once you kick that bad habit, or once you settle down, or once you have a better routine, or once you meet your future spouse, or once you [fill in the blank]. Regardless of where you are in life, God's plan involves you making the right decisions right now. Why wait until later to start being the person that God made you to be right now? Do it now.

It will only be harder in the future, not easier. There will always be excuses. The question is whether you will continue making them or if you are ready to step out in all of your foolish glory. You have everything you need right at this very moment to have peace and accomplish what God wants of you. It won't be easy, but it will be worth it. Start now and don't look back.

Trust God. He made you. He knows what he's doing. Trust him with your future. Trust him with all the honor and glory. Trust him with all the credit for everything good that you do. Do this and you will have more peace and joy than anything in this world can ever give you.

Change will take time, and it's not a onetime decision. So decide now. And then before bed tonight, say yes again. Tomorrow morning, say yes again. If you slip up, get up and say yes again.

Your attempts will not be perfect. You will fail and you will have to try again. Do not lose hope. Such is the temporal struggle of the human experience. Perseverance is the path to perfection. God works wonders in our failure if we're humble enough to let him. And this is only the beginning of an exciting, but bumpy, adventure.

It all starts right now.

God is already with you. He's with you at every step. From the moment you let him in even the smallest crack, he's working in ways you never could have imagined and may never fully know.

Are you ready to begin? He's just waiting on you to say yes. Do you trust the one who made you? Then say yes.

SO HOW DO WE DO IT?

First, let me assure you that the answer is very, very simple — but not easy. It's the answer you don't want to hear because it will mess up your life and all of your plans. And sadly, for this reason, most of us never quite do it.

Jesus describes the answer as two things that include ten thousand. Indeed, we've heard the answer many times before, but it's become so trite that we forget to really consider what is being asked of us. While we do pay it lip service, in practice we quickly pass it over in favor of lesser endeavors that require less of ourselves.

Here are the two parts of the answer:

First: Love God with all your heart, soul, mind, and strength.

We've heard this many times. But have we intensely considered the extent to which we are doing it? Have we grappled with the enormity of that little word *all*?

Loving God is easy. Loving Him with *all* that you are is the work of your life.

And don't forget, loving someone requires giving something of your self. But what can you give someone, like God, who has everything? You give your time and energy.

If you truly love someone, you spend as much time and energy as you possibly can 1) learning about them; 2) talking to them; 3) listening to them; 4) being with them; and 5) serving them. It's not any different with God. If we love God above all other things, that's how we'll spend our best time and energy each day.

Second: Love your neighbor as yourself.

No need to get abstract here. Just love your actual neighbor. I'm talking about the folks who live next door and across the street. Love them. Not just as a mental exercise, like you wish them the best or have good feelings toward them. And not like you make polite gestures toward them when you happen to see them. Actually love them.

But notice that Jesus didn't just say to love your neighbor. He said to love your neighbor *as yourself*. And let's be clear — loving your neighbor as yourself is not just treating people the way you want to be treated when you happen to interact with them.

No! It means that if *your neighbor* has a problem, it's now *your* problem. It means taking on your neighbor's troubles and burdens as your own. It means joining your neighbors in their trenches and being inconvenienced by their problems. It means not just feeling bad for them or understanding their pain, but doing something about it. Love is an action, not a feeling.

More so, this love must be directed at specific individuals, not generalities or groups. Jesus didn't command you to love humanity, but to love individual humans. Not your neighborhood, but your neighbor. People don't need to be loved generally as a whole. They (including your enemies) need to be loved personally, as individuals. They need a true friend. They need somebody who knows them and cares for them personally.

We get so overwhelmed by the number of people who need help, who need to be loved. It paralyzes us. And unfortunately we'd rather sit around and brainstorm social experiments to feed a thousand people than simply go out and feed one person — which each of us could do right at this very moment. And if we did, literally nobody would be hungry.

But that's not really the point. The point is that feeding one person is a thousand times more valuable than feeding a thousand — because it's personal.

Whom does God need you to care for today? Maybe it's the receptionist you pass every morning, a cashier at your favorite morning stop, the UPS guy, the custodian at your building, or a co-worker in the hallway. Maybe it's your next-door neighbor, a person on the train, or a random passerby. Or maybe it's an old friend you too often take for granted.

Look the person in the eyes. Smile. Take time. Remember to ask people about themselves, and then truly listen to their response to see how you can best serve them today.

We must be companions to our neighbors, not tour guides or well-wishers who stand off at a distance, too consumed by our own pursuits and busyness to enter into the lives of others and make them a part of our own.

After all, it is not my truth or your truth we are after. We are after *the* truth. We are not trying to determine *who* is right, but *what* is right. If we seek that as honest companions and care for each other on the journey, we'll not only get there — we'll get there together.

It is that effort, that willingness to go it together for the sake of the other, that true love, that changes the world. Not because it always fixes things, but because it opens people up to seeing the world differently — to seeing each other differently. That's evangelization.

For most of us, though, the neighbors we need to love most are much closer still.

Mother Teresa said, "It is easy to love the people far away. It is not always easy to love those close to us. It is easier to give a cup of rice to relieve hunger than to relieve the loneliness and pain of someone unloved in our own home. Bring love into your home, for this is where our love for each other must start."[10]

Loving our neighbor must not only begin — but crescendo — with the souls in our own home. Yet this can so often be the hardest for us.

We enjoy finding ways to mean a little bit to a lot of people. This is called celebrity. But the real courage lies in daring to become a lot to a little. In daring to be everything to somebody.

This brings us to the final act, the most foolish act of all.

THE MOST FOOLISH ACT OF ALL

So let me go like a leaf upon the water

Let me brave the wild currents flowing to the sea

And I will disappear into a deeper beauty

But for now just stay with me.

— Audrey Assad[11]

The temptation of fame, in all its fashions and forms, has never been greater than it is today. We live in an age when everyone wants a platform, even if it's just a little one. Whether it's on the global stage or a Facebook page, in the classroom or the boardroom, we want our accomplishments recognized. Everyone wants to be known for something. We all want to "be somebody."

But don't let the pursuit of being a little something to everyone keep you from being everything to someone.

There are billions of beautiful people on this planet. And globalization and technology have brought them all within our reach. The temptation, then, when it comes to relationships, is to cast our net wide, experiencing and contributing to as many of the beautiful people, places, and things of this world as we can. And that's a wonderful thing, until it becomes a substitute for the more meaningful and important adventure: going deep.

The human experience, as wide as it is, is much deeper still. You can know a little bit about a billion people and it won't add up to the knowledge you get from deeply knowing just one. It is in the vulnerability and intimacy of our closest relationships that we experience the depth of the human experience.

This is where the most fruitful evangelization occurs, too.

But with our hyper-connectivity, it's easy to spend too much time pursuing the wide embrace of the many convenient, easy relationships and put off going deeper with our most important ones.

We say we love our families, our kids, and our spouses. And we do — but can we do more for them? So many children and marriages aren't getting what they deserve — they aren't changing the world as much as they could — because of our many alternative pursuits. Somehow we're able to keep our minds simultaneously in a hundred different places, yet we've forgotten how to keep them fully present in the moment. We manage to keep up with countless acquaintances, but so scarcely put our all into even one. We so quickly give the world and our work our best, yet struggle just to give our family enough.

Most of us are probably guilty of these things on some level. And I don't think it's because we're bad people. I think it's because we're scared.

We're scared to let go.

We're scared to let go of our need to succeed. We're scared of not getting credit. We're scared of not getting the honor and power that come with whatever career path we're on. We're scared of missing an opportunity. We're scared of having our struggles and achievements go unacknowledged. We're scared of not maximizing our potential and our productivity. We're scared of being alone.

Most of all, we're scared to put everything we have into the few treasured people we've been given, so we instead spread our love and interest among many. We're scared to go deep, so we go wide. That way we always have somebody without ever having to risk everything.

But if you want to live a life fully alive, you must risk everything. It is the only way to find your peace and your place in this world.

It's time to dig deep and find the courage to detach ourselves from all the meaningless metrics of the world so we can pursue what truly matters most. It's time to do what Jesus is asking us to do. It may look foolish to the world, but in the end, it will be the only thing that mattered.

You will do small things with great love. You will do big things for a great few. Nobody else may know about it. This is how we evangelize the world.

It may not be sensational or entertaining. It won't be easy. It probably won't bring you fame. Your life might look ordinary to everyone else. It might mean that the legacy you had planned for yourself is very different. Nobody else in the world may ever hear of you or know about you . . . except for the folks who matter most: your family and friends and, yes, your neighbor.

But as you do this, something magical happens.

Because as you let go of pleasing the many, it allows you to grab hold ever more firmly of the few who need you most. As you become small to the world, you are more free to love as a giant. In an extraordinary way, you again become most present to the people God has placed into your life in a special and direct way.

It's time to stop taking them for granted. It's time to dive deep, reveling in the infinite significance of the closest, precious relationships you've been given.

What we need are husbands and wives who put more into their marriages than they do their careers. We need mothers and fathers who put more into their kids than they do their hobbies. And we need neighbors who put more into each other than they do their social activism.

When we do all of this, eventually we fall in love completely. We become so effortlessly in love with God and at the service of one another that we forget ourselves completely.

Jesus wasn't telling us a riddle when he said, "Whoever finds his life will lose it, and whoever loses his life for my sake will find it." He was plainly spelling out the secret to life: Dare to let go.

Let go and fall deeply into your magnificent place in the world. When you begin to live in this way, shoving all of your selfish interests aside, you begin to see the simple and miraculous life God planned for you. You become truly free to do the right thing, to respond to Jesus' simple commands and to become the only "somebody" you ever needed to be. It may even feel like you're disappearing from the world and missing out, but you're not. You're disappearing into a deeper beauty.

In time we are able to step back for a better view of our life. And then we start to see that all along our messiness was really a part of a much greater order. That all of our foolishness was a part of a much deeper beauty. We are each just a few short, rough paint strokes that make up a tiny part of a beautiful masterpiece. Find your place within it and shine. This is true happiness.

That is what it means to be right where you're supposed to be. This is how we evangelize the world. This is what it means for your heart to rest in him, you beautiful and foolish mess. Now go.

"If you are what you should be, you'll set the whole world ablaze." — St. Catherine of Siena

WHAT'S NEXT?

Join the movement at
MessyAndFoolish.com where you can:

- take the Messy & Foolish Challenge

- hear some messy & foolish stories

- download a very messy, foolish
  and short study guide for groups

- watch some interviews with some
  messy & foolish people

- or receive other free messy & foolish
  essays from Matthew

NOTES

1   C. S. Lewis, *The Weight of Glory and Other Addresses* (Grand Rapids: Eerdmans, 1965), 113.

2   Peter Kreeft, *Fundamentals of the Faith: Essays in Christian Apologetics* (San Francisco: Ignatius Press, 1988), 203.

3   *Gaudium et Spes*, no. 43.

4   Benedict XVI, "New Technologies, New Relationships: Promoting a Culture of Respect, Dialogue, and Friendship," Message of the Holy Father for the 43rd World Communications Day, Sunday, 24 May 2009.

5   See G.K. Chesterton, *St. Francis of Assisi*, in *The Collected Works of G.K. Chesterton*, Volume 2 (San Francisco: Ignatius Press, 1986), 30.

6   Catholic News Service interview published in part in the Argentine weekly *Viva*, July 27, 2014. http://www.catholicregister.org/faith/item/18548-pope-francis-reveals-top-10-secrets-to-happiness.

7   Peter Kreeft, "How to Win the Culture War"
    (audio talk, lecture, given multiple times in
    different venues); http://www.peterkreeft.com/
    topics-more/how-to-win.htm.

8   The words "one wild and precious life" can be
    found in the Mary Oliver poem, *The Summer
    Day* in *New and Selected Poems* (Boston, Mass.:
    Beacon Press, 1992).

9   Paraphrased quote from *A Serious Call to the
    Devout and Holy Life*, William Law (Fig Books,
    2012), Kindle edition.

10 *Love: A Fruit Always in Season: Daily Meditations
    by Mother Teresa* (San Francisco: Ignatius Press,
    1997) p. 129.

11 Audrey Assad and Sarah Hart, "Show Me"
    (River Oaks Music Company BMI, 2010).

THE
DYNAMIC CATHOLIC
INSTITUTE

[MISSION]

To re-energize the Catholic Church
in America by developing world-class
resources that inspire people to
rediscover the genius of Catholicism.

[VISION]

To be the innovative leader in the
New Evangelization helping Catholics
and their parishes become
the-best-version-of-themselves.

DynamicCatholic.com
Be Bold. Be Catholic.®

The Dynamic Catholic Institute
5081 Olympic Blvd
Erlanger, KY 41018
Phone: 859-980-7900
info@DynamicCatholic.com